Skelfie's Spookeville

Lola and the Halloween Mischief

By

Lilli Adams

Skelfie's Spookeville

© Copyright 2025 - All rights reserved.

The content contained within this book may not be reproduced, duplicated or transmitted without direct written permission from the author or the publisher.

Under no circumstances will any blame or legal responsibility be held against the publisher or author, for any damages, reparation, or monetary loss due to the information contained within this book, either directly or indirectly.

Legal Notice:

This book is copyright-protected. It is only for personal use. You cannot amend, distribute, sell, use, quote or paraphrase any part of the content within this book without the consent of the author or publisher.

Disclaimer Notice:

Please note the information contained within this document is for educational and entertainment purposes only. All efforts have been executed to present accurate, up-to-date, reliable, complete information. No warranties of any kind are declared or implied. Readers acknowledge that the author is not engaged in the rendering of legal, financial, medical or professional advice. The content within this book has been derived from various sources. Please consult a licensed professional before attempting any techniques outlined in this book.

By reading this document, the reader agrees that under no circumstances is the author responsible for any losses, direct or indirect, that are incurred as a result of the use of the information contained within this document, including, but not limited to, errors, omissions, or inaccuracies.

Lilli Adams

Dedication

This book is dedicated to intergenerational relationships and to one very special and much-loved Poppy who laughed out loud at his own jokes.

Acknowledgment

This book acknowledges children's rights to be playful, creative and to have fun. We acknowledge diverse cultural practices and hope that sharing in each other's traditions and customs brings joy.

Lilli Adams

Skelfie's Spookeville

Skelfie's Spookeville

Lola, the miniature dachshund, lived a happy life with Grandma and Grandpa. She had a cozy bed, lots of toys, and a big yard to explore. But Lola wasn't just any dog—she was cheeky! She loved hiding Grandpa's slippers under the couch and unrolling Grandma's yarn.

Lilli Adams

One October, Lola's favorite time of year, the grandchildren came to stay for two whole weeks! They always brought extra cuddles and belly rubs, which Lola adored. Her tail wagged as she greeted them, giving each a slobbery kiss.

Skelfie's Spookeville

Lola wasn't allowed to eat the sweets they were making for Halloween, but that didn't stop her from sniffing every corner of the kitchen, hoping for crumbs! While Grandma baked and the kids decorated, Lola "helped" Grandpa in the yard by burying her chew toys.

Lilli Adams

One afternoon, Grandpa opened a dusty box. Inside were plastic jack-o'-lanterns, orange lights, and a rubber bat missing a wing. At the very bottom, wrapped in tissue paper, was something special.

"Say hello to Skelfie!" Grandpa said, holding up a little skeleton toy dressed like a ringmaster. His stitched grin looked almost as cheeky as Lola's.

"This was your uncle's favorite Halloween toy," Grandpa explained. "Legend says Skelfie gets up to tricks when no one's looking!"

The kids giggled. "Like Lola!"

Lola sniffed Skelfie, her tail wagging. He smelled like an adventure waiting to happen.

Skelfie's Spookeville

That night, curled up in her bed, Lola couldn't sleep. She knew the truth: Skelfie wasn't just a decoration—he could move! She'd seen him sneaking around before with his tiny, bony hands.

This year, Lola made up her mind. She'd catch Skelfie in the act and prove he was the real trickster.

But little did Lola know, Skelfie had plans of his own—and Halloween was about to get a lot cheekier!

Lilli Adams

The next morning, Lola stretched in her cozy bed and noticed Grandma and the boy heading to her kennel. Curious, she trotted after them, tail wagging.

Grandma pointed inside the kennel, and the boy gasped. "My socks!" he exclaimed, pulling out a scrunched-up ball of fabric.

Lola tilted her head. She didn't remember putting the socks there! She gave her best innocent puppy eyes, but the boy frowned. "Lola, why did you steal my socks?"

Lola whined. She didn't steal them! But how could she explain?

Then, out of the corner of her eye, she saw him—Skelfie! The little skeleton peeked from behind the kennel, his cheeky grin wider than ever. Lola barked to get their attention.

"Lola, hush," Grandma said. "They're just socks."

Grandma and the boy went back inside, leaving Lola sitting in front of the kennel, frustrated. She knew Skelfie was the troublemaker!

This time, she decided, she'd catch him in the act. No more getting blamed—Skelfie's tricks were about to end!

Skelfie's Spookeville

The next day, Lola woke up to more commotion. Grandma and the boy rushed outside, sounding surprised. Curious, Lola scampered after them, her ears bouncing.

At her kennel, the boy gasped. "My toys!" he cried, pulling out two action figures.

"Lola," Grandma said, "why are you taking the boy's things?"

Lola tilted her head, confused. It wasn't me, she thought, but how could she explain?

Then, she spotted it—a shiny stick behind the kennel. Skelfie's ringmaster cane! Skelfie stood perfectly still, pretending to be a regular toy, but his grin was as cheeky as ever. Only Lola noticed his tiny wiggle, teasing her.

Lola barked and pointed her nose at the stick. Look! It's him!

The boy frowned. "Lola, stop taking my stuff!" He carried his toys back inside.

Lola huffed, sitting in the grass as they left. Skelfie popped up and twirled his stick like a showman. He gave a cheeky bow before disappearing around the corner.

Lola's tail drooped. How would she prove Skelfie was the real troublemaker?

Skelfie's Spookeville

The next day, Lola woke from a mid-morning nap, ready for more Halloween fun. She heard voices outside and trotted over to see. Behind her kennel was the big Spookeville Circus sign Grandpa had painted.

"Why would Lola hide this?" the boy frowned.

Grandpa shook his head. "How could a little dog move such a big sign?"

Lola barked, trying to say, *It wasn't me!* Nose to the ground, she sniffed for clues—and spotted him.

Skelfie! Perched by the fence, leaning on his Ringmaster stick, his grin as cheeky as ever.

Lilli Adams

Lola growled, giving him her best *I know it was you* look. She barked again, louder, but Grandpa just laughed.

"Oh, Lola, always barking at nothing," he said.

The boy sighed, picking up the sign. "Let's put this back, Grandpa."

Lola sat in the grass, frustrated. How could they not see Skelfie was behind it all?

The little skeleton gave her a cheeky wave before disappearing behind the fence.

Lola's tail wagged with determination. This time, she'd catch Skelfie in the act and show everyone the truth!

Skelfie's Spookeville

Lola could feel it: Halloween had arrived. The air smelled sweet, pumpkins and spiderwebs were everywhere, but Lola wasn't happy. She still hadn't stopped Skelfie's tricks.

Small accidents happened throughout the day. Light strings became tangled, candy disappeared, and Grandpa's top hat ended up in Lola's bed. Each time, Skelfie's cheeky grin was nearby.

Lilli Adams

That evening, the yard transformed into the Spookeville Circus. Lola, in her lion costume, nervously wagged her tail beside the boy in a ringmaster jacket.

"Welcome to the Spookeville Circus!" Grandpa announced.

The crowd cheered, but then something magical happened. Skelfie jumped onto the stage, twirling his stick.

Skelfie's Spookeville

"And now, for our grand act!" he said in a tiny voice only Lola could hear. "Lola, the daring lion, jumping through a hoop!"

Skelfie pointed to a sparkling hoop. Lola ran as fast as her little legs could go and soared through, landing perfectly. The audience roared with applause.

As the show ended, Skelfie tipped his tiny hat, giving Lola a proud nod.

That night, curled in her bed, Lola thought about the magical day. Maybe Skelfie wasn't so bad after all. As she drifted off, she heard a tiny whisper:

"Good job, Lola. Until next year…"

The End

www.ingramcontent.com/pod-product-compliance
Lightning Source LLC
Chambersburg PA
CBHW061227070526
44584CB00029B/4023